GW00456714

Living your values

Team Leadership Standard 2021

Pete Ashby & Krysia Hudek

Copyright © 2021 Pete Ashby & Krysia Hudek
All rights reserved.

ISBN: 9798585353710

"No part of this publication may be reproduced, distributed, or transmitted in any form or by any means, including photocopying, recording, or other electronic or mechanical methods, or by any information storage and retrieval system without the prior written permission of the publisher, except in the case of very brief quotations embodied in

Contents

Welcome

We very much hope that you find our Team Leadership Standard useful as a framework for supporting your team in working more closely together in 2021.

TEAM**2030** is a UK-based leadership think tank that we founded in the early weeks of our first national lockdown in 2020.

Our mission is to support leaders in building more unified and agile leadership teams that can help them better realise their shared ambitions as we all hope to leave behind the awful Coronavirus pandemic.

The general propositions in ***Living your values*** come from the thousands of hours that we have both spent supporting all sorts of leadership teams moving forward in their journeys "from good to great".

Living your values is also much inspired by the wisdom of those business leaders and entrepreneurs who act as our TEAM**2030** Influencers.

They worked up the breakthrough behaviours with us through a series of in-depth consultations, constantly drawing on their own leadership experiences to fine-tune the behaviours as we moved forward.

Our Influencers include some of the most accomplished leaders in the UK and we are both incredibly grateful for their ongoing guidance and support. Their details are on our website: www.team2030.co.uk.

Pete Ashby & Krysia Hudek

The Team Leadership Standard

Everyone in a leadership position in any sort of organisation recognises the importance of team working. We learn about this mainly through our experiences of what happens when team working goes wrong!

When things get really bad, the Chief Executive calls the team together and reminds everyone that they are meant to be "singing from the same song sheet".

People agree to get on better with each other, and then a little further down the track something else goes wrong again and the team is called in for another pep talk!

Even where the organisation has a strong balance sheet, this might well be **in spite of** the ways in which members of the top team behave towards each other.

Almost without exception, the successful teams that we have worked with have a keen sense that they could be a lot better than they are.

Those that "walk the talk" a lot more than most are invariably the first to say that they need to find new ways of living their values more fully.

Really successful, high performing top teams that are there for each other are in the minority.

This is largely because it is genuinely tough for a team to develop an agreed sense of what they stand for and a shared belief about what it **means** to live their values.

"Good to great" for leadership teams

We see *Living your values* as a 2021 version of good to great for senior leadership teams that recognise that the future of their organisation will depend to a significant degree on how much they support and champion and challenge each other as a team.

The Standard sets out a series of 14 stretching leadership behaviours based on our core values of trust, purpose, curiosity, connection, humility and courage.

Each behaviour draws on at least **two** of these values and has the potential to create a significant step forward for teams that already work together fairly well and want to become a lot better.

This is why we call them breakthrough behaviours.

A self-assessment tool

We invite Chief Executives to use ***Living your values*** as a self-assessment tool to support them in ramping up their performance as leaders and leading by example with a greater sense of confidence and purpose.

We hope that once leaders have assessed themselves against the Standard they will wish to share it with their immediate team and invite them to adopt some or all of these behaviours as their **own** Leadership Standard.

An organisation-wide framework

The idea is that as the top team draws on these behaviours to improve their own standards of performance, Directors will wish to go through the same sort of process with their own teams.

They can explain which breakthrough behaviours the top team find most useful for themselves, and then ask their team to choose the ones that work best for them.

In this way, we hope that ***Living your values*** will gradually be adopted by members of different teams and offer an organisation-wide framework for team leadership development.

Delighting in difference

We hope that as you read the breakthrough behaviours you will find that a number of them could help with bringing your corporate values to life.

We expect that whilst some of the behaviours might strike you as stretching others might make you think, *"That's easy, what's the problem?"*

Our experience has been that pretty well all of us are likely to feel challenged by some of these behaviours and comfortable with others. This is why we want to encourage you to focus on those behaviours that challenge you the most, on the basis that they should support you the most in your development as a leader.

As for those that you regard as easy, please remind yourself that some other members of your team might well find them difficult, just as they might have no problems with taking on one or two that you find rather challenging.

Support and mentoring

We hope that you will regard the process of working through ***Living your values*** as an opportunity to take stock of the standards of support that you offer each other in your team.

Please see yourself as a source of support and informal mentoring for those team members who say that they are most challenged by one or two of the behaviours that are second nature to you.

You might, say, be able to agree a reciprocal arrangement with another member of the team and support them in adopting a behaviour that they find challenging and you find relatively straightforward. You might then swap roles in relation to one that you find quite a lot harder than they do.

Let yourselves delight in difference!

Pause and reflect

You will see that at the end of each breakthrough behaviour we include a section for your personal notes, with the heading 'Pause and reflect'.

When we were developing ***Living your values*** with our TEAM**2030** Influencers, we were struck by their different approaches towards assessing themselves as they considered the questions introducing the breakthrough behaviours.

These discussions underlined for us the importance of individuals and teams working through the behaviours in a way that is most useful for them.

Some people like to rate themselves out of 10 as their quickest way of differentiating between those behaviours where they are strongest and those where they're weakest.

Others like to mark the behaviours according to how drawn they are to them.

They might write in *'yes'* at the top of this space for one that they favour and see themselves as practising, and *'no'* for one that they dislike.

In the case of behaviours that they endorse and would like to practise more fully, they use phrases such as *'to work on'*.

We have both lived with most of these behaviours in our minds for a long time, and our response to a number of them is a single phrase: *'work in progress'*.

Please make this Standard yours

Whether or not you decide to score yourself in terms of how much you already practise each behaviour, or how drawn you are to them, we hope you will make this Standard yours as much as possible.

We also hope that you will sometimes use the prompt of 'pause and reflect' to do just that. So many of us don't do this nearly enough.

The 14 breakthrough behaviours

To what extent do you...

Our six values

Before considering these breakthrough behaviours, we first want to introduce our six core values because they provide the context within which we have come to focus on these particular behaviours.

In drawing out at least two values that underpin each of these breakthrough behaviours, we are not seeking to imply that it is the same values that drive these behaviours for all of us.

For different leaders, key behaviours will draw on different values that reflect their personal story as well as their own understanding of the requirements of their current leadership role.

Trust

The first value is that of trust. All successful teams recognise that high levels of trust are at the heart of how they work together.

Without mutual trust, it is only a matter of time before some sort of external challenge results in members of a team turning against each other. With trust, anything is possible so long as the team reminds itself that this gift is fragile and can never be taken for granted.

Trust is especially powerful when it combines with connection, as for example in the breakthrough behaviour (number 8) when we make a point of asking others to treat our word as our bond.

Deeper levels of trust open the door to deeper levels of connection that itself makes possible deeper trust.

Purpose

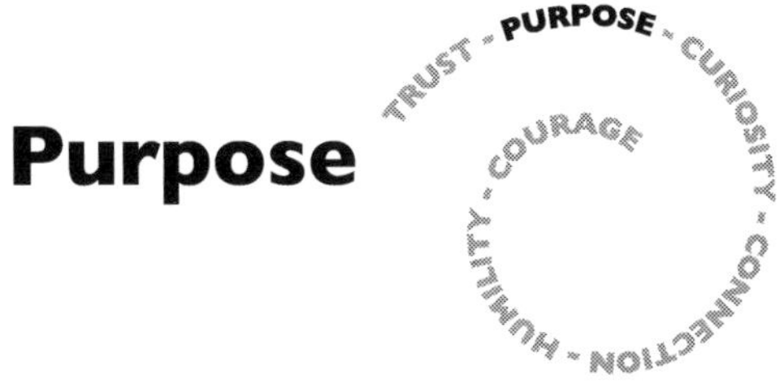

For top performing teams, one of the greatest unifying forces that they share is their sense of common purpose.

For some it is so strong that you literally sense it within seconds of being in the same room as them.

It is no surprise that a number of the most challenging breakthrough behaviours require leaders to draw on this value of purpose in order to move forward.

For example, our breakthrough behaviour of not postponing difficult conversations (no 12) often draws on the two values of purpose and courage.

Those who have a habit of avoiding difficult conversations find the courage to speak up and risk some difficult things being said for the sake of the organisation's higher purpose.

Curiosity

Our value of curiosity brings to mind Albert Einstein's famous words, *"I have no special talent. I am only passionately curious."*

Passionate curiosity is nearly always at the heart of a team that stands out as special. It reflects the passion for learning that team members share with each other: their passion for their core business as well as their passion to understand better why others think in the ways that they do.

Our breakthrough behaviour about inviting and offering verbal feedback (no 13) draws heavily on this value of curiosity, whilst combining it with that of purpose.

The impact of the two values together can be quite transformational for relationship-building, as more and more leaders are discovering by inviting informal feedback as a natural part of their daily conversations with colleagues.

Connection

We have already pointed to the immensely powerful bond between trust and our core value of connection. So it probably won't surprise you that the breakthrough behaviour referred to by some as "connect not convince" (no 6) also combines connection with trust.

Of all the leadership behaviours that we have explored in depth with different Chief Executives and leadership teams, this one stands out as the single most transformational behaviour when a top leader takes it on as part of their commitment to living their values.

During the Coronavirus pandemic the value of connection has been particularly weakened in so many teams, as they have not shared the same physical space for months on end. Many now need to make a special effort to establish deeper connections if they are to achieve the performance breakthroughs they are looking for.

Humility

Our next core value is that of humility. One of the difficulties with this term is that some people associate it with religious notions of unworthiness. In using this word we wish to uncouple it from this and instead emphasise the importance of humility in situations where we feel valued for what we have to offer as leaders.

Our breakthrough behaviour about owning our weaknesses as well as our strengths (no 2) is a good example of what this value of humility can make possible for a team.
It also shows how humility can link up so powerfully with trust.

Taken together, these two values enable leaders to talk in a relaxed way about those areas of work where they would like to be able to offer greater support to others and also those where they would appreciate greater support because others are naturally more talented.

Courage

The final core value that is so essential to effective team working is that of courage. Courage is one of those virtues that can come in a burst and in almost a single moment take us across a threshold that we couldn't expect to cross without this act of courage.

Many of us need to draw on our sense of courage if we are to take on board our breakthrough behaviour of asking colleagues for help (no 3). As we go on to discuss, many leaders seem to have persuaded themselves that this is something they are not allowed to do once they reach a certain level of leadership.

In this case, leaders show vulnerability by drawing on the values of courage and trust. In the process, they almost certainly build greater connection too, because others can receive it as such an affirmation of what they have to offer for another member of the team to ask them for support.

Exploring the breakthrough behaviours

1-14

1 To what extent do you continually challenge your own ways of thinking?

If your answer is *"quite a lot!"*, you will know that this principle of self-challenge is really fundamental to becoming that much more consistent in leading by example.

Permitting ourselves to challenge our own assumptions requires us to have high levels of trust and confidence in ourselves as leaders.

It also requires us to have a strong sense of our purpose as leaders. This is so important if we are to remain focused on our core business mission and avoid becoming distracted by side dramas that can result in us tripping up over the "baggage" that we have acquired as part of life's journey.

As we challenge ourselves we draw on our inner curiosity. Our curious self is part of our self-challenger, prompting us to ask ourselves tricky questions time and again.

Commitment to connecting with others

We so value high levels of connection and believe profoundly that going into an argument with an open mind is of much greater value than going into an argument aiming to win it.

We know that sometimes we can get drawn into over-arguing on behalf of a particular position. In these moments, our commitment to connecting with others as well as our desire to show humility make it easier to tell our "inner barrister" to take a break so that we can listen a little harder!

We also know that self-challenge is an attitude of mind that doesn't exempt us from the leadership responsibility to take clear decisions, often at short notice and sometimes with huge unknowns attached to the decision.

What it does mean, though, is that if we subsequently suspect that we got the decision wrong we should at least be able to hear some tough truths and ask how we can get back on track.

Our humility and courage combine to enable us to listen to others telling us things that we really don't want to hear.

Diversity of thinking

Another powerful dimension to self-challenge is the extent to which it promotes diversity of thinking within a team.

The simple fact that team members have diverse backgrounds and identities doesn't of itself ensure diversity of thinking.

Diversity of thinking requires an outward-going mindset that involves us rejoicing in difference and constantly seeking to learn from each other.

This reinforces a culture in which we feel able to be ourselves and wish others to feel the same way too, whilst at the same time coming ever closer together as one unified team.

Pause and reflect

Continually challenging yourself

2 To what extent do you let yourself talk about your strengths and weaknesses in a relaxed way?

We intentionally start with Chief Executives because it is the CEO who creates the culture of their top team, and it's the top team's culture that influences the ways of working of every other team in an organisation.

This is one of those behaviours where the role of the CEO in leading by example is crucial to determining the behaviours adopted by other Chief Officers and Executive Directors.

CEOs who fail to acknowledge their own strengths make it very difficult for those around them to do so.

The same goes for discussing our weaknesses. If a CEO does not feel able to be open about their weaknesses, with all the authority they can take for granted in their position as Chief Executive, how can they expect those who work for them to show the honesty they don't feel able to demonstrate themselves?

More and more CEOs now recognise that leading by example requires them to be up-front with their team about those aspects of their leadership where they are not so strong as well as those where they are strong.

Vulnerability

For those CEOs who resist the idea of acknowledging any shortcomings of their own, one of the reasons often given is that this would make them "vulnerable".

The term here implies that rather than being a good thing, vulnerability could result in any recognition of weaknesses on their part being used against them to undermine their position.

We know that many leaders have real difficulty with the idea of making themselves "vulnerable" with professional colleagues.

Some have spent years believing that this would be interpreted by colleagues as a sign of their lack of fitness to do their job. They find it a struggle to regard vulnerability as desirable and affirming, even when there are already high levels of trust.

This can be incredibly hard for some, which is why it is so important that others offer encouragement when a colleague shows vulnerability in sharing something about themselves.

Vulnerability within teams nearly always builds trust. It also demonstrates our readiness to show some humility as we affirm our commitment to living our values.

Tough questions

This raises tough questions about the degree of candour that leaders should expect to show towards others and receive in return.

The number one question that vulnerability and candour raise is of course about trust.

We can't expect team members to be relaxed about discussing their strengths and weaknesses in advance of experiencing a high level of mutual trust with others round the table.

Vulnerability and candour become transformed from risks into natural features of high trust relationships, once the levels of trust reach a certain height.

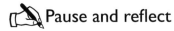

Pause and reflect

Owning your strengths and weaknesses

To what extent do you feel able to ask your colleagues for help?

It sounds easy, doesn't it. Asking a colleague for help.

What's so special about that? Actually, rather a lot!

The simple truth is that many leaders seem to have persuaded themselves that if they ask for help they will somehow be exposing themselves to be inadequate as leaders.

We have both experienced all sorts of fears of inadequacy over the years and have coached many different leaders who have their own fears of inadequacy.

So widespread is this fear that when one of us meets a leader for the first time we tend to ask ourselves not so much **whether** they will have any fears of inadequacy but rather **what** are their particular fears of being exposed as an 'imposter'.

Personal fears of this sort can result in many leaders persuading themselves that they are expected to be entirely self-sufficient.

If you are reading this and thinking "That's me!" you might also be thinking that this is a pretty deep-seated instinct of yours and it's going to be hard to change a mindset that you might have had for some years.

It might well have its origins in your family's culture and some significant role modelling in your early years that resulted in you associating this idea of not asking for help with proving that you can stand on your own two feet!

A role model for others

One of the most effective ways of freeing yourself from this fear of inadequacy could be to remind yourself that you now need to act as a role model for others in your team.

Do you want them to be able to ask for help when they feel out of their depth for some reason and would benefit from some sort of peer support?

Assuming that you want to lead by example, this can offer a strategy for helping to manage yourself.

Self-empowerment

You tell yourself in no uncertain terms that if others are to feel empowered to ask for help as part of their commitment to their own wellbeing, you need to show that you have a sufficient sense of self-empowerment to role model this behaviour too.

Whenever we feel that we must somehow meet all of our needs as a leader, alone and unaided, we can do ourself a big favour by remembering our commitment to ask for help.

So please think again if you are one of those people who believe that by asking for help you would be demonstrating inadequacy on your part in a way that you're not allowed to do as a leader.

Making it more difficult for others

As well as making leadership more burdensome for yourself than it needs to be, not asking for help also makes it difficult for others to ask for help when they most need it.

If it's so difficult for you, how can you expect it to be any easier for them?

If you have managed to persuade yourself over some years that you're not really meant to ask for help, you will almost certainly need to show some courage to get yourself to do what you have told yourself you're not allowed to do.

It can help a lot if you start by telling a close colleague that you are finding something rather difficult and would appreciate their support with it.

Then ask your question and let yourself be aware of how they clearly enjoy the fact that they are able to give you some support.

Letting go of a self-limiting behaviour

In asking others for help you are letting go of the absurd fantasy that a good leader somehow needs to do their job to the standard required of them entirely on their own.

You deploy courage and trust to let go of a self-limiting behaviour and at the same time let someone else demonstrate that it means a lot to them to be able to support you as a leader.

Pause and reflect

Asking for help

To what extent do you champion members of the team in ways that affirm their distinctive specialness?

This is one of those behaviours that is so dependent upon the Chief Executive modelling the behaviour if it is to become commonplace among the leadership team.

Where the CEO avoids championing others, it is still possible for other team members to take on this role. It can help a lot if at least two members of the team share this role until it becomes a natural part of the dialogue among the team.

Championing other members of the team takes many forms.

Sometimes it might involve singling them out for praise for a specific achievement, or just acknowledging the way they made something happen.

At other times it might involve teasing them appreciatively for how they have achieved a success in their own unique way!

A force to be reckoned with

Championing involves you "seeing" and acknowledging other members of the team in ways that capture their distinctive specialness.

A team whose members affirm and champion each other is without doubt a force to be reckoned with.

 Pause and reflect

Championing others

To what extent do you show curiosity before letting yourself challenge colleagues' ideas?

This behaviour is all about us drawing on our curiosity in order to connect as much as we can with others' thinking.

Before voicing any disagreement with what someone else is saying, we first show some curiosity to try and understand why they think as they do. We are conscious of our tone and body language as we ask a question to hear some more about the other person's thinking, as a sign of our genuine interest in what they have to say.

This is why we need to show we are listening hard as they respond to our question. Our intention is to role-model the behaviour that we want them to adopt towards us.

So if the other person says they don't want to consider anything other than their own idea, we are able to assure them that we will take it away and reflect on it.

At the same time, we hope they might have a chance to think a little more about the approach that we have put forward.

Building a two-way connection

The fact that we constantly demonstrate a real and genuine curiosity and are keen to engage with the other person's thinking should make it easier to build a two-way connection between us.

 Pause and reflect

Showing curiosity before offering any challenge

To what extent do you connect with others' ideas and hold back from convincing them that you are right?

Our hope is that you will consider this breakthrough behaviour as a team and reflect on how you handle the discussion with each other as some of you – perhaps – say that you are drawn to it and others say that you are far from persuaded.

Simply put, this behaviour insists that there is a world of difference between asking others to accept that you are right and asking them to share their thinking with you on the basis that you're open to being persuaded that you are wrong and they are right!

This reminds us of the importance of the principle that the Standard here is **yours**! This is essential if you are to connect with others' ideas to a greater extent and hold back rather more from trying to persuade them that you are always right.

Connection rather than persuasion

In order to achieve this, it needs to be about your ambition to place a higher value on connecting with the viewpoints of others in your team rather than persuading them to support yours.

The standard-setting sits in how you behave towards each other in the moment and then how you feed back the ways in which your thinking has moved forward after a little time to reflect on what others have said.

We all know colleagues who can find themselves uttering the words *"I disagree with that!"* or *"You are wrong!"* when someone else is just half-way through their first sentence introducing a fresh idea. We must admit that as well as thinking of some colleagues when we say this we also think of ourselves!

Over the years we have done this with each other more times than we can imagine. Nowadays when one of us slips back into this old habit the other one will burst out laughing and ask in a teasing way, *"Where's your curiosity gone today?"*

Utterly different

The reason "connect not convince" has felt so exciting when we have discussed it with different teams is because it is utterly different from how most leaders believe they are meant to behave once they have their seat at the top table.

So many have become senior leaders with an assumption in their minds that to show themselves worthy of becoming a Chief Officer or Vice-President they need to have a keen view on just about any topic that comes up for discussion.

They need to "know their own mind" and demonstrate confidence and clarity of thought at all times.

From this standpoint, it is only too easy to develop a habit of over-arguing on behalf of what we believe to be right.

This is why it is so important that where a team decides to take on "connect not convince" as a shared habit, members agree to remind each other of this – gently - when they find themselves over-defending a particular position, as they are bound sometimes to do!

No imaginary steam-roller

The maxim of connect not convince means that if and when we explain why we don't agree with the other person, our primary aim is not to prove them wrong.

Rather, it is to share with them why, having heard their thinking behind their proposal, we are still not convinced that they are right and therefore want to hear some more from them to understand their thinking better.

The proposition here is that the prize of achieving a greater connection with others far outweighs the benefits that we can sometimes gain by going hard out to win an argument and managing to trounce any possible opposition from within the room within a few minutes.

When some CEOs hear about "connect not convince" they assume it means that if others disagree with them they are obliged to **keel over** and not do what they believe to be right.

Nothing could be further from the truth.

Doing the right thing

We believe fundamentally that all leaders should do what they believe to be right.

Sometimes it might well be the "right thing" for a Chief Executive to follow a particular course of action even if every other member of their leadership team believes that this would be a mistake.

Leaders all have to make up their own minds about what they believe to be the "right thing" to do.

What this particular breakthrough behaviour challenges is the habit of climbing into an imaginary steam-roller and driving straight at someone who disagrees with what is being proposed.

Where others signal that they're not persuaded by what we have to say, let us show some curiosity, and some humility too, and enter into a conversation on the basis that they might be right and we ourselves might be wrong.

Being truly heard

We have both often found ourselves in situations facilitating Board and Executive team awaydays where those in a minority position on a key debate about strategy have been more than happy to defer to the view of the majority, so long as they feel they have been listened to and truly heard.

Pause and reflect

Seeking to connect rather than convince

To what extent do you try to stand in the shoes of colleagues in different work settings?

We all recognise that the social and economic consequences of the Coronavirus pandemic will be with us throughout most of the 2020s.

Future business success will depend crucially on our ability to empathise with the hopes and fears of colleagues in different work settings and with different patterns of working from our own.

It is so important that we don't under-estimate the extent to which the bonds among team members and between different teams have been weakened by Covid-19.

After so long communicating with each other via Teams and Zoom, many teams have become more fragmented as personal loyalties and connections have been weakened.

Loss of connection

In some sectors there has been a worrying polarisation between many "front line" workers, who have had to expose themselves to the danger of being infected with Covid to travel to work to do their job, and many knowledge workers who have been able to work entirely digitally from the comfort and safety of their own home.

It is so important that teams are honest with each other about the widespread loss of connection during successive lockdowns.

It is no surprise that many of those leaders with a low level of empathy before the pandemic found their empathy levels dipping still further, as they engaged with colleagues from within their particular 'postage stamp' on the screen.

From the safety of their home it was easier to respond defensively to messages they didn't want to hear, knowing that if others persisted all they had to do was turn off their camera whilst claiming they had a poor internet connection!

A challenge to our levels of empathy

Going forward, millions of workers will find themselves developing more "blended" patterns of working, combining varying amounts of digital homeworking from home with working from their office or a workplace hub.

At the same time, there will be growing numbers of full-time homeworkers as well as significant numbers of employees who continue to be based full-time at one place of work.

In this context, it will be more important than ever that we each try to stand in others' shoes as a vital part of the process of reaffirming the importance of connections and mutual understanding both within and between teams.

For all of us, this will pose a challenge to our levels of empathy.

Everyone will have to work that much harder to try and maintain high levels of personal connection with each other, from wherever they are working.

Pause and reflect

Standing in others' shoes

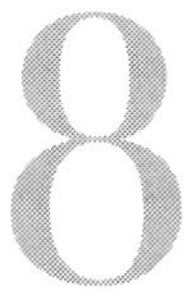

To what extent do you regard your word as your bond?

In high trust teamworking, there is surely something very powerful about the principle of "my word is my bond".

This phrase is a sign of team members taking themselves seriously in the best sense possible.

They know that when they say they will do something, they have entered into an obligation that matters.

If they subsequently find that they need to withdraw from this obligation, this will have to be handled in a way that is fully transparent and respectful of the fact that they have let down others who were rightly expecting them to follow through on their previous promise.

This culture of honesty at all times is founded on the principles that the truth always comes first and every member of the team assumes the best of the others.

These two principles are at the heart of our understanding of trust and fundamental to driving connection.

Putting their integrity on the line

From this starting point, everyone recognises that whenever they make a promise they are putting their integrity on the line.

For teams that are constantly challenging themselves, life is constantly moving on. So the promises that we make to each other are part of a wider process of movement and high trust connection.

None of us should be surprised when something that we have "promised" works out very differently from how we intended. In these moments, it is our sense of integrity and our commitment to absolute transparency that need to shine through.

When we give people our word as leaders, it doesn't really mean that we promise solemnly to achieve x by y date with z benefit to our bottom line.

Rather, it means that we will go all out to achieve this and if it looks as if we're not going to land it, they will hear this from us before they hear it from anyone else.

No wish to cause a "wobble"

We so value our team's respect for our integrity that we will go to very considerable lengths to avoid any surprises that could give them cause to have a "wobble" about the extent to which they can rely upon us always acting with integrity.

We are people of our word because our word is our bond.

We are collaborative, collegiate and open. We are open about risks and dangers as much as about prizes and benefits.

We don't play down bad news and don't hype up good news.

We do what we say and say what we do.

Sometimes we get things wrong and have to put our hand up and apologise.

Sometimes we achieve more than we hoped for and in these moments we always pay tribute to those who made this possible.

Pause and reflect

Treating your word as your bond

To what extent do you embrace collective responsibility and support all decisions made by your team?

When we were discussing key breakthrough behaviours, we were at first rather hesitant about including this one. Some of our TEAM**2030** Influencers challenged us, *"Isn't this obvious?"*

Sadly, we know that the answer for a lot of teams is that when members don't agree with the outcome of a discussion they tend to say rather little about it – or, worse still, make a point of dismissing its importance - when they report back to their own team.

There is a wide expectation among many extended leadership teams that if their own team leader doesn't agree with a decision taken by the top team, they won't make any particular effort to help make a success of it. They might go along with it, but they will find their own way of signalling to those in the know that if anything goes wrong they themselves were more than sceptical from day one.

When teams act in this way, they are actually breaching four of our core values all at the same time: trust, purpose, connection and humility!

The starting point for curiosity

To us, the essence of top performing teams is that people say what they believe to be right for their organisation in terms of its wider purpose.

They also trust the fact that others have the organisation's best interests at heart as much as they do.

It is this proposition that provides the starting point for curiosity about why others might think differently.

It means that in situations where members of the top leadership team find that they are in a minority position when a decision is taken, they show the humility to embrace collective responsibility and advocate the decision as fully as anyone else.

Because they made a point of getting inside the thinking of those who advocated the winning position most enthusiastically, they are able to explain why the decision was taken in a really positive way.

Also, their sense of commitment to their shared purpose tells them that so often what matters most is not the specific decision that was taken but the spirit in which it is taken forward by everyone concerned.

We all know how a "not so good" decision carried out with a real sense of positive purpose can generate a better outcome than the so-called "right" decision carried out with resentment on the part of some that the course of action that they favoured was overlooked.

No need to pretend to agree

Collective responsibility does not require leaders to pretend to agree with something they don't agree with. It requires leaders to be very clear in spelling out why a course of action is being taken and demonstrating that they are as committed as anyone else to making a success of it.

It can reinforce the sense of integrity of a top team for a leader to say that they were not all of one mind, but at the end of the day most people felt that this was the best option on the table and now every one of them is going all out to achieve all that they are hoping for.

No single right thing to do

There is no cynicism and no sense at all of anyone withholding approval.

There is just a straightforward statement that after a healthy debate a clear course of action has been agreed and everyone is getting behind it.

Everyone knows there will be times when teams are at odds about "the right thing to do", because so often there is no single right thing to do and top performing leaders care a huge amount about trying to do the right thing.

So all high performing teams will occasionally have healthy disagreements and maybe the occasional flaming row behind closed doors!

Once a decision has been taken, everyone is out there doing all they can to make sure that what they're collectively responsible for is a winning decision.

They all accept their shared responsibility for taking forward whatever has been decided with one voice.

This is the point about collective responsibility.

Whatever anyone might or might not have said **before** the decision, all that matters is what everyone does once the decision has been taken.

If you are proved right

For those teams that adopt our first breakthrough behaviour, you know that your commitment to self-challenge is ongoing.

It embraces all that you do.

This makes it easier for any who believe that the decision taken was wrong to follow it through wholeheartedly.

You know that if you are proved right **someone else** will almost certainly say something to you first without you having to say a thing!

Pause and reflect

Embracing collective responsibility

10 To what extent do you hold yourself accountable to your team?

In asking this question, we're thinking of you as a team member who is **not** the Chief Executive, because we know that many CEOs would say that they're accountable to their Board through their relationship with their Chair.

So we're thinking of you as a Chief Officer or Executive Director and asking to what extent you see yourself as accountable to your top leadership team led by the CEO.

We can imagine what some of you are thinking. Just as the Chief Executive is accountable to the Chair, so am I accountable to my CEO!

If we pause and reflect on this for a few seconds, it's easy to see why so many top teams have such a problem with their sense of identity as a team.

For a lot of top teams, the truth is that when Chief Officers and Executive Directors join the table for a team meeting, they do so on the basis that their primary relationship is with the Chief Executive.

Peer relationships are secondary

Their relationships with their peers around that table are of secondary importance to them. And when we say of secondary importance, the truth is that in many cases these peer relationships are not nearly as important as their relationship with their CEO.

If you are a CEO and think that you want your Directors to feel a primary loyalty to you, the challenge surely is to try and achieve this without sacrificing openness and genuine debate at team meetings in the way that so many CEOs have done.

Of course the bilateral relationships between a CEO and individual Directors are incredibly important, and of course it is sometimes best that the CEO uses this one-to-one space to discuss specific concerns they might have about under-performance on the part of an individual Director.

Our point is that as well as investing in these bilateral discussions, CEOs and Directors need to invest energy – and risk - in making sure that as a team they discuss up-front the really "tough stuff" that they know is getting in their way.

Too few make this commitment, and as a result too many agendas for top team meetings are far too impersonal and transactional.

"Super managers" rather than Directors

The Directors end up being treated like a bunch of "super Managers" rather than as a bunch of Directors.

Wouldn't it be good if more top teams could develop their meetings in such a way that Directors naturally share with each other how they think they are performing, and feel free to ask each other for help in those areas where they have got behind in driving progress towards the team's agreed priorities.

From the standpoint of the CEO

So, let's think about this from the standpoint of the CEO, because this is surely one of those areas where a CEO initiative could make such a difference.

Let us imagine that as CEO you are having a team discussion that involves a review of performance since the Board meeting the previous month.

It's all rather low key and everyone is being fairly cautious and defensive.

In the midst of this you say that for various reasons you didn't give as much attention as you should have done to one of the key action points that you were taking forward from the Board meeting.

You took your eye off the ball and as a result are quite some way behind compared with where the Board expects you to be.

You would really appreciate it if one or two of the Execs would give you some support with this over the next couple of weeks so that you can get up to speed in time for the next Board meeting.

In this moment you have actually just acted on three breakthrough behaviours in one go, given that you have owned a weakness and asked for help (behaviours 2 and 3) as well as holding yourself accountable to your team!

Most important, you have shown some real honesty and vulnerability with the team.

Impact on team culture

Coming from you as CEO, this very statement is bound to have quite an impact on the culture of the team going forward, not least because it should make it considerably easier for others to follow suit.

It would be so easy for you to build on this at the next meeting, by thanking the team for the way they responded and also saying that you want to be very clear going forward that when mistakes are volunteered in a spirit of learning, this should be seen by everyone else as an affirmation of the power of the team.

As you all experienced, this act of volunteering reinforced openness within the team as well as the team's shared commitment to your wider purpose as an organisation.

Being held to account

This means that it would also be a great time to say that you wouldn't be happy if a member of your team failed to volunteer a significant mistake within the high trust atmosphere of a team meeting.

Moreover, it would be unacceptable if anyone were to go so far as to conceal a mistake.

The principle here is fundamental to us all living our values. It isn't just about openness, important though that is in its own right.

It is about individual leaders being held to account for the consequences of their actions.

Self-accountability

In practice, accountability works at a number of levels, since we are accountable to ourselves as leaders as well as to our line manager and our team.

What is so empowering about self-accountability is that it frees us up to share with others our concerns whenever we feel we've under-performed.

If we already push ourselves hard they won't be surprised, because they know that those leaders who believe most keenly in self-accountability tend to set the highest possible standards for themselves.

In the process of holding ourselves to account, the values of personal standard-setting, trust, humility, vulnerability and courage all come together as one.

The energy they can create is truly exceptional.

Pause and reflect

Holding yourself accountable

11 To what extent do you call out unhelpful behaviours in the moment?

How many times have we all been part of a meeting, either physically or on-line, and then said later to someone who was part of it, *"Let me tell you what I nearly said ….?"*

Surely no-one wants to be a leader who nearly said something and didn't, only to store it up and use it as a complaint about someone else at a moment when they're not in a position to respond!

Whenever we feel that a colleague is exhibiting an unhelpful behaviour we need to find a way of calling out that behaviour so that they hear our challenge before anyone else does. This can take some courage, especially for those of us who are quite conflict averse!

What we do know is that the longer we delay before we say something that we regard as "difficult", the harder it is for us to make sure that the tone is light and warm.

Now isn't the right time

We have all experienced times when we have held on to something for too long, so that when the words come out of our mouth they rather sound as if they have been pulled out from the back of a store cupboard and almost thrown at the other person!

It really is remarkable how we can persuade ourselves not to say something because now isn't the right time. The longer our postponement goes on, the more we can insist to ourselves that in holding back we are showing caring. We're just waiting for the right moment to say what we want to say.

Even if that moment comes and we manage to speak our truth with a perfect tone, we might find ourselves asked **exactly when it was** that their behaviours caused us the concern that has led us to say something now.

If we say something like *"three weeks ago"* or *"last month"* or even *"last year"*, we know that the passage of time will have created a whole new problem to do with trust.

"So you waited all this time to tell me? You've clearly stored this up and said nothing. It's as if you've been lying to me, pretending that everything is fine whilst harbouring a grudge against me all along. How can I trust you now?"

Said with kindness

When we challenge the behaviours of colleagues, three incredibly important words are "**in the moment**".

If we can't challenge their behaviours there and then, we should say something as soon as possible afterwards.

It is so much better to refer back to a meeting that took place yesterday rather than one that took place last week or last month.

As well as seeking to call out unhelpful behaviours in the moment, we should always call them out with kindness, in our tone as well as our words.

The kinder we are, the easier we make it for the other person to receive our challenge as offered in the spirit of assuming the best.

Said with kindness and in the moment ... these few words count for so much, as well as truly being a challenge for us all.

Pause and reflect

Calling out unhelpful behaviours in the moment

12 To what extent do you initiate difficult conversations that may make you and others feel uncomfortable?

Our starting point is that there are times when we all need to work at finding the courage to open up a difficult conversation, even when we know that this will make us and others feel uncomfortable.

If and when we hesitate, we ask what will best serve our wider purpose. The very fact of asking this question can help to give us the confidence we need to press ahead and say what we believe needs to be said.

For the truth is that teams that don't feel able to discuss difficult issues together are teams that impose their own "glass ceiling" over their development as a team.

In the process of trying to summon up the courage to speak our truth, it can help a lot to remind ourselves that teams that achieve their shared purpose "travel light" and deal with difficult issues as they arise.

High trust working doesn't spare us!

A lot of us try to avoid difficult conversations not only at the level of the team but also in our one-to-one relations with colleagues.

In those moments when we are on the look-out for excuses, there is one group of people that some of us are only too ready to take off our list of potential candidates for a difficult conversation. We think of those close colleagues we trust the most and tell ourselves that we can spare ourselves any sort of difficult moment with them.

No need for that, since there is so much trust between us already. Phew!

If something happens that causes us to have a "wobble" in our relationship with a close colleague, we are in danger of deceiving ourselves if we imagine that the level of trust between us will protect us from the wobble.

In practice, the high level of trust between us might well result in the wobble knocking us off balance even more!

Showing courage

In this situation, it is so important that we take the risk of opening up a conversation that could prove to be difficult.

We tell the other person what it was that threw us and then draw on our curiosity to ask whether they were thrown by the situation as well.

We explain that we value the trust between us too much to let something jeopardise it in any way.

We are sure that if we discuss this now and don't let it sit and fester, we will find that either there was a misunderstanding between us that we can easily get over or else there was an honest difference of opinion.

We share our wobble and in the act of doing so acknowledge the specialness of our relationship with this individual.

In taking the risk of having a difficult conversation with a trusted colleague, we definitely show courage.

Then once the conversation is underway curiosity becomes our great ally.

It gives us the best possible chance of finding out how the other person experienced our reaction to the situation as well as how they reacted themselves.

Pause and reflect

Not postponing difficult conversations

13 To what extent do you invite - and offer – verbal feedback as a natural part of daily conversation?

So many leaders are happy to complain about the culture of their organisations being too passive and top-down.

Yet they often don't accept their own responsibility for modelling the feedback behaviours essential to an organisation becoming more dynamic and bottom-up.

Part of the problem is that when many leaders think of feedback, they immediately think of themselves offering feedback to their direct reports about their performance and not of inviting others to give them feedback about their own development as a leader.

This is no surprise, because many of us still tend to associate feedback with formal processes of appraisal and review, in which line managers give feedback to those who report to them about how they have performed against their targets.

It is very natural that individuals who have experienced this sort of feedback over some years should hesitate when they hear this word being used by their line manager.

They just have to think of one moment when they had to defend themselves against unfair criticism of their performance and they are bound to feel on the back foot!

From judgement to development

If leaders are to draw on feedback as part of their organisational mission to become more creative and agile, they need to uncouple the word 'feedback' from formal appraisals in which individuals are often expected to justify their behaviour.

Instead, they need to link it to informal conversation in which the feedback is developmental and genuinely two-way.

They need to stress that they will always want to view any criticism as offering genuine advice and support to benefit their development.

This will need to be said more than once to those who fear that they might end up being penalised if they speak their mind only to find that the person inviting feedback then resented what they heard!

A continuing dialogue

To encourage others to take risks in what they say, leaders need to stress that they most want to hear about any behaviours of theirs that might be getting in the way of them continuing to develop as a leader.

Through ongoing feedback offered in a spirit of truthful generosity, curiosity and purpose reinforce each other in ways that enable everyone involved to feel more listened to and empowered.

The key word in this sentence is **ongoing**.

It takes the focus away from one particular sentence that might contain a difficult message and refocuses on a continuing dialogue over days and weeks between two individuals committed to each other's development as a leader.

Pause and reflect

Inviting and offering verbal feedback

14 To what extent do you show kindness to yourself as a leader?

All of these breakthrough behaviours raise tough challenges for all sorts of leaders in leading by example.

The reason we include this final behaviour is because there are so many leaders who find it incredibly difficult to be kind to themselves in the process of facing these challenges!

Please be kind to yourself as you assess yourself against this Standard and encourage others to approach it in the same spirit.

All high performing teams have a shared capacity for pushing themselves and keeping on moving forward to try and reach for the stars.

What a lot of high performing leaders are not good at is showing some generosity of spirit towards **themselves** in those moments when they slip back.

Showing forgiveness - towards ourselves

Imagine how strengthening it would be to feel that you are developing together as a team and sharing insights with each other in a kind way.

When we use this word kind, we don't mean that you just say nice things to each other! It's vital to talk openly and honestly about those areas where you've got some things wrong as a team and have lessons to learn.

To be able to achieve this, many of us in leadership positions need to show a little more forgiveness towards **ourselves** in moments when our performance is not up to the mark.

We sometimes need to remind ourselves that mistakes offer us great opportunities to learn and grow, and can become real **gifts** so long as we view them with the right mindset.

This involves us asking some tough questions and also showing kindness towards ourselves and others as we reflect on our answers.

Honesty, stretch and kindness

Honesty, stretch and kindness: between them, they offer three key features of a team that has the capacity to become unstoppable.

All the time, the honest sharing of ideas and the generous championing of others are about enabling the team to stretch itself further, to go the extra mile and experience the excitement of limitless possibility.

Pause and reflect

Being kind to yourself

Limitless possibility

Stretching yourselves more

Behind all 14 questions in this Standard, there is one that we have not set out in a heading because it is in many ways a constant from beginning to end:

How much are you there - really there - for each other as a team?

The teams that are growing and developing together at pace should be able to say, without pausing for breath, *"More than ever"*.

Once you feel you can say this, you know that the possibilities for yourselves as a finely tuned orchestra - or jazz band - playing outstanding music team are limitless. How exciting is this!

If you are to step into these areas of limitless possibility, you and other members of your team will need to commit to stretching yourselves more and more. We hope this Team Leadership Standard will support you in doing just that.

Please help us stretch this Standard!

On our website, www.team2030.co.uk, we have posted a number of videos to support you in using ***Living your values*** to help develop your top team.

We will constantly update them as we work with CEOs in using this Standard as a tool for team development.

In keeping with the spirit of **Living your values**, we are committed to continually challenging ourselves about how to make it more useful for senior leadership teams.

We would so appreciate it if you would let us have your feedback about how we can make ***Living your values*** work better for you.

Every January we will publish a revised version, incorporating some fresh breakthrough behaviours that we will develop together with our TEAM**2030** Influencers and CEOs adopting the Standard.

If you were redrafting the Standard and wanted to make it more effective for top team development, what else would you want to cover – and is there anything in particular that you would leave out?

If you have any suggestions, please give us your thoughts in an email to **pete@team2030.co.uk**. Pete will get back to you directly.

Your three top action points

In the meantime, how about capturing three top action points or resolves for yourself on the next page?

If you have used this as the basis for a discussion with your team, perhaps there are some **team resolves** that it would be good to capture as well.

Just a few phrases are usually enough to remind you of what you need to do to ensure that you and your team step forward more confidently and truly *live your values*.

Top action points & resolves

About us

We first worked together in the late 1980s when Pete was a Fellow of St George's House, Windsor Castle and Krysia joined him as a facilitator.

In the 1990s we went on to run strategy and ideas-building sessions together for senior leaders across the private, public and third sectors, with "no hidden agendas".

After 9/11, Krysia also became a Fellow of St George's House and concentrated on national work with Boards and top teams.

At the same time, Pete led an intensive series of international events in Windsor Castle on global trust-building and conflict resolution.

From then on we ran all sorts of leadership development events for teams as well as offering 1-2-1 coaching to CEOs committed to improving their performance as leaders.

In 2016, Pete was invited by the Board of St George's House to set up the Society of Leadership Fellows in Windsor Castle, building up a fellowship of 250 leaders from every sector of the UK and a range of other countries.

Krysia took on responsibility for developing the format for the Society's Leadership Conversations. Together we worked up new processes for leadership development based on creating a safe space for self-challenge and high trust peer support.

After the Castle closed its gates due to the Covid-19 lockdown in March 2020, we established TEAM**2030** and invited a range of top leaders we have worked with over the years to join us as Influencers.

We will be working as a team to develop ***Living your Values*** as a truly international Team Leadership Standard.

As it evolves, the Standard will always be designed for CEOs leading winning teams that constantly set themselves higher standards - and **aim to exceed them**.

Printed in Great Britain
by Amazon